Usui Reiki Level 4 Manual

Master - Teacher

Level 4: Shihan

By
Nicolas ORLER

Translated by
Joffrey BOURDET

Proofreading
Séverine DELANOIS

Level 1: Shoden
Level 2: Okuden
Level 3: Shinpiden
Level 4: Shihan

Graphic legend

Icons	Meaning
📖	Noteworthy
△	Warning!
💣	Forbidden!

Introduction

Welcome to the world of Usui Reiki Master teachers, in the lineage of Mikao Usui. In the first three levels, we focused on physical, mental and conscience healing. We also worked on expanding our consciousness, both spiritually and on the level of the subtle worlds. In Level 4, we will be working almost exclusively on the protocols needed to initiate students on all four levels.

With time, practical exercises and a lot of diligence, we gradually absorbed each level. I congratulate and thank you for your beautiful perseverance. However, you may have slightly modified certain processes, by force of habit, during your interventions, whether voluntarily or not. In principle, this poses no problem for healing others, whether privately or professionally, as long as your intentions remain benevolent and sound.

But when teaching others, you must scrupulously respect the various processes and exercises. As an Usui Reiki Master, you must be beyond reproach, both in your teaching and in the various initiation processes of your students. There is nothing very complicated about this: all you have to do is follow the teachings presented in the four levels of my manuals.

I know this may seem a somewhat rigid position, but it is the only way to preserve the philosophy of traditional Reiki and the sacred character of transmission. Consequently, it will allow you to establish your credibility as an Usui Reiki Master teacher.

1 Symbols used to initiate Levels 1 to 4

1.1 Symbols known from Level 2 and Level 3

HON SHA ZE SHO NEN (HSZSN)
Symbol of distance and connection

To free yourself from time and space, from distances, no matter how long. To connect with a person, a situation.

SEI HE KI (SHK)
Symbol of harmony (both mental and emotional)

To harmonize dualistic or conflictual situations. To cleanse behaviors that are not beneficial to us. There is an element of protection against difficult emotions, low vibrations that are spiritually destructive.

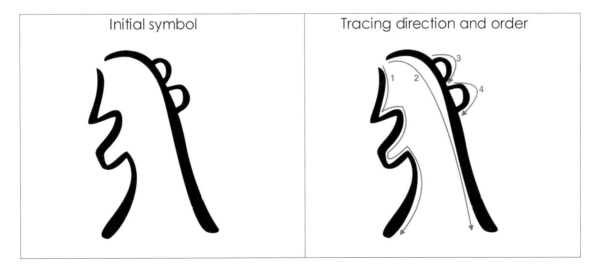

CHO KU REI (CKR)
Symbol of power and focus

To bring all the energy to a point of focus, whether physical or not, and seal it there.

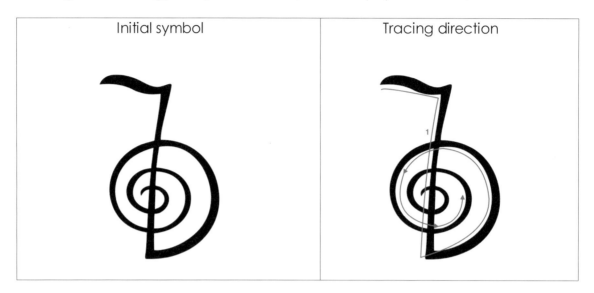

Initial symbol	Tracing direction

Shi Ka Sei Ki (SKSK)
Symbol of heart

The energy of this symbol has a heart-opening effect, something we all need to do. It helps us to live a better relationship of true Love, both with ourselves and with those around us, with great benevolence.

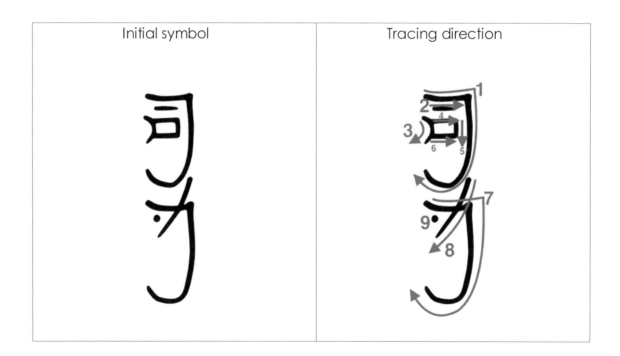

Initial symbol	Tracing direction

Dai Ko Myo (DKM)
Master symbol

Dai Ko Myo is a key to supreme consciousness, leading to spiritual awakening and self-realization. Or to the light of ultimate wisdom.

Initial symbol	Tracing direction and order

1.2   New symbols

1.2.1   Tibetan Dai Ko Myo (TDKM)
Master teacher symbol. Symbol of expansion of spiritual awareness.

1.2.1.1   Role
The Tibetan Dai Ko Myo does not replace the Usui DKM. It is used during initiations (during the "Violet Breath", which we will look into later). But it can also be used to great advantage during treatments. It primarily affects the spiritual dimension of the recipient, whether in a face-to-face, distance or self-treatment setting.

It invites divine energy to expand and penetrate our consciousness, like a godlike funnel. Incidentally, this funnel idea is strongly suggested in its calligraphy.

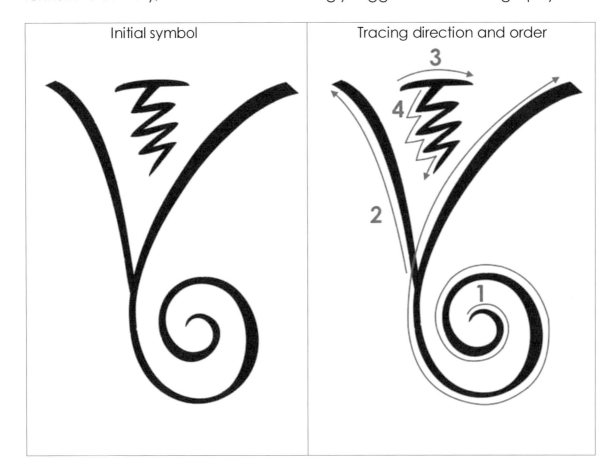

Initial symbol	Tracing direction and order

1.2.1.2   Use
Like all other symbols, it is activated by pronouncing its mantra three times (Dai Ko Myo). It can be used to treat others (either face-to-face or distance healing) or oneself. Please note that this symbol is drawn from the bottom (starting with the spiral).

Throat symbol

Acts on the throat and the upper respiratory tract.

1.2.2.1   Role
Whether the ailment is physical or subtle, this symbol can be used to treat ailments in and around the throat.

For the physical part: for treating a sore throat, certain thyroid problems, scalene muscles, frontal parts of the trapezius, etc... Refer to the anatomical plates in the Level 1 manual.

For the subtle (energetic) part: as we have known since Level 1, the throat has its own chakra. The throat chakra is linked to our inner and outer communication. It can be interesting to activate this symbol before speaking in front of a group of people, for example. Or simply to get in touch with our inner self or inner child.

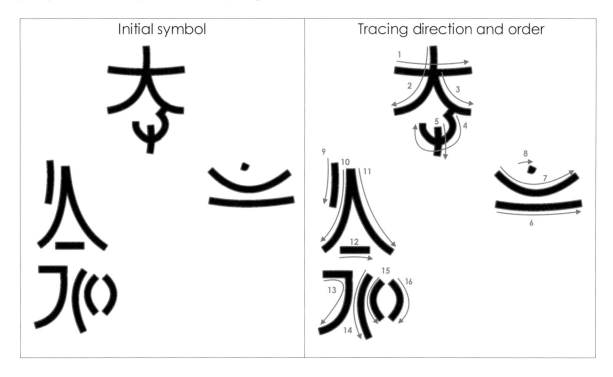

Initial symbol	Tracing direction and order

1.2.2.2   Use
Like all other symbols, it is activated by pronouncing its mantra 3 times (Chi Ka So: CKS). It can be used to treat others (either face-to-face or distance healing) or oneself. It is beneficial to use this symbol if you want to communicate with your inner self or, more poetically, with your soul.

Symbol of chakra alignment and initiation. Mantra: "Serpent of Fire" (SF)

1.2.3.1   Role
To treat back problems and to initiate a student with the Violet Breath (see Violet Breath chapter).

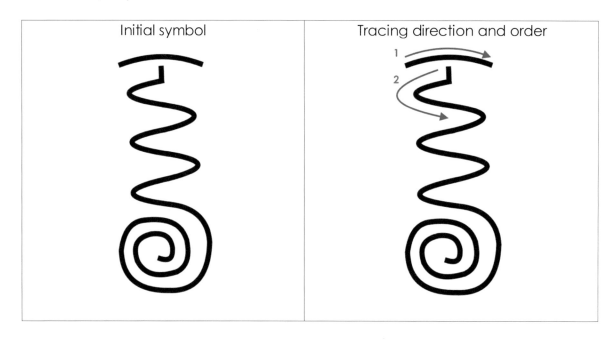

Initial symbol	Tracing direction and order

1.2.3.2   Use
For initiations: on the back. See the Violet Breath chapter.
For treatments: in front of the body. The Serpent of Fire helps to align the chakras and needs to be done even before the aura scanning (Byosen, from Level 2), and then as often as we feel fit.

In both cases, we do not touch the body. As a matter of fact, the spiral is traced in front of an intimate area of the person. The upper curved line (drawing 1) is drawn at the top of the head, and the vertical line goes down along the back of the neck (or along the throat if we are facing the front of the body), the wavy part is drawn evenly along the back (or along the front of the upper body) and the last spiral ends at the base of the spinal column (sacrum) or at lower abdomen level. (+ mantra 3 times)

Back symbol. Mantra: "Dragon of Fire" (DF)

Note that the Dragon of Fire mirrors the Serpent of Fire (SF).

1.2.4.1 Role

Treatment of back problems or back pain.

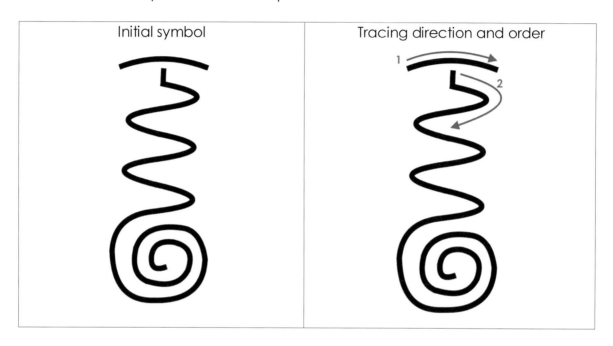

Initial symbol	Tracing direction and order

1.2.4.2 Use

Trace it over the entire back. Then activate it with your mantra (3 times)

We do not touch the body, as the spiral is also drawn in front of an intimate area of the person. The upper curved line (line 1) is drawn at the top of the head, the vertical line along the nape of the neck, the wavy part spread evenly across the back, and the final spiral completes the symbol at the base of the spinal column (sacrum).

2 A message to the new Master teacher

Becoming a Master teacher gives you the opportunity to teach others. However, this important, newly-acquired skill comes with important new responsibilities!

Yes, I can already see some of you smiling. But this statement does not come from a Hollywood movie. This quote was first used in speeches and addresses made by Franklin D. Roosevelt in 1945, and even earlier, in 1906, by Winston Churchill (one of the next British prime ministers): *"Where there is great power, there is great responsibility."*

In other words, by becoming a Master Teacher in the lineage of Mikao Usui, you agree to initiate others according to the founding principles and philosophy of the sacred Japanese Sutras (books). It was he who rediscovered these 2500-year-old Sutras. He then decided to pass on their teachings.

At this point, it is worth remembering that these age-old traditional teachings are highly sacred, conferring subtle knowledge and powerful healing skills and tools.
Forgotten over time and distorted by some, this therapeutic and consciousness-enhancing knowledge is now unveiled to the world, but it has not lost its sacred and valued aspects.

However, the Internet, the media, the detractors of anything outside of hard sciences and other supporters of rational skepticism are trying to demonstrate the ineffectiveness of such energetic practices, or even worse, to relegate them to the rank of sectarian actions. Unfortunately, we cannot disagree with them when we look at the accomplishments done by some Reiki practitioners.

This is why I am speaking to you:
- Pass on your knowledge with sincerity and honesty, while respecting the sacred ancestral discretion observed by the original teachings.

- It is not some kind of gift that you inherited: you have relearned what has been forgotten for millennia. But you have worked much harder than others.

- You are not superior or more important than your students: but they listen respectfully to your words as you are someone who knows things, someone who is able to help them on their initiatory journey.

- Do not let your ego or your brain overpower your benevolence and your love of others. Instead, you need to reconnect with your childlike soul, your confidence in life.

- You have not become a Guru: you are lucky and honored to be able to pass on your knowledge with great wisdom and discernment.

- By remaining upright, sincere and honest every day with others and yourself, your soul becomes stronger, and shines around you like a jewel.

May the creative Source fill you with its benevolent light!

3 Pre-requisite knowledge before initiating the student

3.1 Contraction of the Hui Yin (perineum)

Regardless of gender, the Hui Yin is an energy reservoir located between the genitals and the anus. Physically, it consists of the muscles, tissues and ligaments of the perineum, an ensemble shaped like a small hammock or pouch. It is also known as the pelvic floor.

Generally speaking, while women naturally find it easier to grasp its precise location and function (childbirth, contractions, etc.), men often use it too, but without realizing it.

Apart from its intense involvement during lovemaking, it supports the organs located in this area (bladder, uterus, rectum), contracts the vagina, and ensures urinary and fecal continence, without us always being aware of its action.

For further clarification, the pelvic floor is mainly made up of two paired muscles: the levator ani muscles and the coccygeus muscles. These muscles sit on the pelvis minor, forming a muscular diaphragm on which the pelvic organs rest (mentioned above).

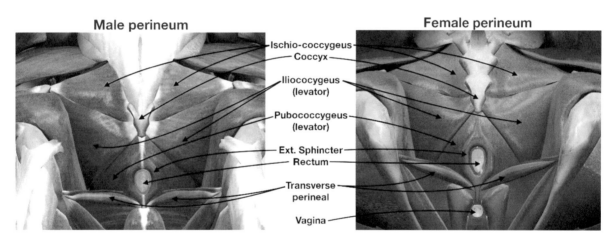

Male perineum · Female perineum · Ischio-coccygeus · Coccyx · Iliococygeus (levator) · Pubococcygeus (levator) · Ext. Sphincter · Rectum · Transverse perineal · Vagina

During initiations, we must use it and contract it. To practice contracting it —and without going into the details of the less-than-glamorous aspects of the human being— let us say that we consciously contract it when we are holding back a pressing urge, or when we are desperate to avoid flatulence in public (in other words, when we need to relieve our bladder or release the gas from our intestines).

I invite you to practice contracting it before continuing with your students' initiations. It is important to know that during initiations, we need to contract the perineum for several minutes. It is worth noting that, naturally, the first initiations are not always easy due to the lack of training, which means the initiation time is de facto lengthened. So you need to practice beforehand.

3.2 Violet Breath

The Violet Breath is an important step common to all four main initiations. It is supposed to be perfectly assimilated by the Master before any initiation, and be acquired knowledge at this point.

1. We stand behind the person, both hands on the crown chakra, eyes closed.

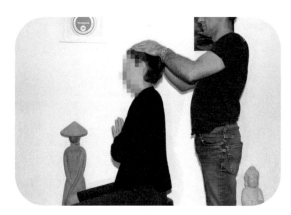

2. We contract the Hui Yin. **It will remain so until the end of the initiation.**

3. We place the tip of the tongue on the junction between the teeth and the upper gum.

4. We inhale deeply and calmly through the nose, while visualizing the Reiki flow coming to our crown chakra, going down along the front of our body to reach the perineum (Hui Yin) and passing between our legs. Then, while breathing out, the flow goes up behind the back and accumulates towards our head.

5. In our mind, we visualize this energy as a white cloud rotating clockwise. The cloud gradually changes color, tending towards purple (if it helps, you can imagine passing through all the colors of the rainbow before settling on purple).

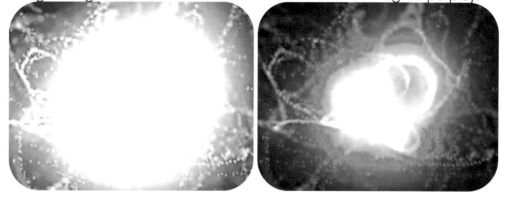

6. Let us visualize the Tibetan DKM penetrating this cloud, without activating the symbol (with its mantra) for the time being.

In this image, the DKM appears in black for better visibility, but imagine it as white (or gold) as possible.

7. Then all at once, without interruption:
   o We open our eyes.
   o We lean forward, towards the top of the student's head.
   o We blow energy (gently and without loosening the tongue from the teeth) on the top of the student's head, while visualizing the cloud with the Tibetan DKM coming out of our mouth and into the person's head.

8. Let us visualize this purple energy (with its symbol) completely penetrating the student's head, curling up at the base of the skull (beginning of the nape of the neck). With our dominant hand, we "follow" this downward movement towards the nape of the neck.

9. Let us activate the symbol with its mantra (DKM 3 times): if that helps, we can lightly touch the back of the neck and utter the DKM mantra 3 times to activate it.

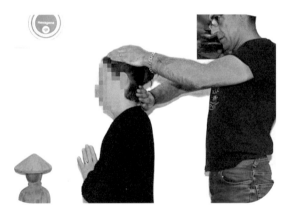

3.3 Breath of Life

The Breath of Life is also an important step in all four initiations. And likewise, the Master should be completely familiar with this technique before any initiation.

Standing in front of the student, about three feet away:

- We trace a CKR with the tip of our tongue (without detaching it from our teeth/upper gum), or we trace it mentally on the tip of our tongue. Then we activate it with by saying its mantra 3 times.

- We blow towards the student, in one continuous breath:
  1. On their hands (joined in the Gasshô pose).
  2. We go down towards solar plexus level.
  3. We work our way up to the top of the head.
  4. We go down again towards solar plexus level.
  5. Then, we finally come back to the hands.

A mnemonic technique: when blowing energy on the different areas, we trace a sort of squashed "W" shape:

Top of the head			3		
Hands	1				5
Solar plexus		2		4	

3.4 Symbol organization

For easier reading and to make the initiation procedures smoother, we will organize the nine symbols as follows:

Mantra (symbol)	Acronym	Order	Western translation
Hon Sha Ze Sho Nen	HSZSN	1	Connection/distance
Sei He Ki	SHK	2	Protection/mental/emotional
Cho Ku Rei	CKR	3	Power/strength/to seal (consolidate)
Shi Ka Sei Ki	SKSK	4	Heart symbol
Dai Ko Myo	DKM	5	Master symbol, Usui Reiki
Chi Ka So	CKS	6	Throat symbol
Dragon of Fire	? (DF *)	7	Back symbol
Serpent of Fire	? (SF *)	8	Back / upper body / alignment / initiation
Tibetan Dai Ko Myo	TDKM	9	Master symbol, Tibetan Reiki

📖 *** The abbreviations for the Serpent of Fire and Dragon of Fire symbols do not exist in any official or recognized Reiki methods. But for easier reading and understanding of this course, we will simply shorten them "SF" and "DF". This system only exists within the frame of this manual.**

Conventionally, symbols are used in the following order:
> During a treatment: 1 2 3 5 4 6 7 8 9.
> During an initiation: 9 8 7 6 4 5 3 2 1.

But in this course, we will study the symbols in this order:
> During a treatment: 1 2 3 4 5 6 7 8 9.
> During an initiation: 9 8 7 6 5 4 3 2 1.

<u>For treating others or oneself:</u>
> Symbols come to us in an intuitive or haphazard way, so there is nothing compulsory about this and nothing forcing us to apply them all in the order listed above, even if we must recognize that the order set out above follows a certain logic. We do not have to use every symbol for every treatment either.

> It also seems quite clear that Usui Reiki has become more and more rigid over time (whether intentionally or not). But these four courses (these four manuals) follow the philosophy that we can do no harm with Reiki as long as our intentions are sincere and benevolent. The method only works if it appeals to us. Otherwise, constraining ourselves to it would be useless and even counterproductive.

📖 **Feel free to follow your intuition and your feelings; they will be all the more beneficial for you and the recipient.**

4 Preparation for the Master and the initiation site
Connection, cleansing, vibration enhancement & protection
4.1 Master preparation

In Level 4, we will complete this preparation by tracing the Tibetan DKM beforehand:
1. Gasshô pose.
2. Connect to the student's Reiki Source & express your intention of protection and purification ("I ask for your protection and to be purified by your light...").
3. Ask your guides for assistance ("I call upon my guides, I ask for...")
4. Full Kenyoku.
5. Trace a Tibetan DKM in the palms of both hands.
   Clap your hands 3 times, each time uttering your mantra.
6. Trace an Usui DKM in the palms of both hands.
   Clap your hands 3 times, each time uttering your mantra.
7. Trace a CKR (Cho Ku Rei mantra) in the palms of both hands.
   Clap your hands 3 times, each time uttering your mantra.
8. Draw a CKR (+ its mantra 3 times) on each of the 7 chakras, one at a time.
9. Gasshô pose and gratitude for having this request granted.

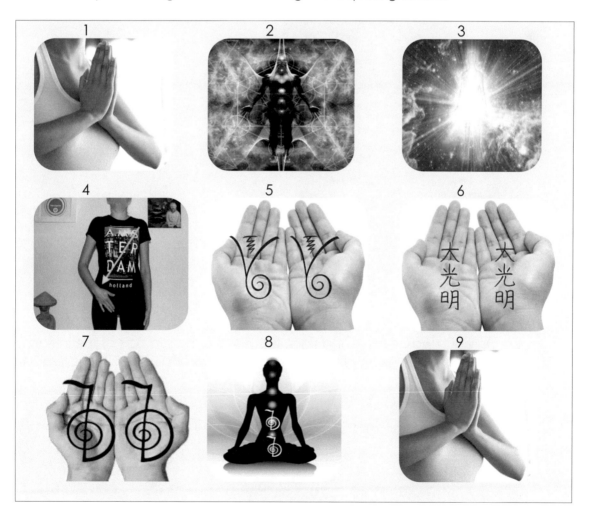

4.2 Site preparation
Creating a sacred, protected space

1. Let us trace the following symbols in the space (i.e. in the air) of the initiation site:
   TDKM, SF, DKM, CKR, SHK, HSZSN. Activating them one after the other by pronouncing each corresponding mantra 3 times.

2. On each wall, ceiling and floor, let us trace the symbols of the initiation site:
   SHK and CKR —activating each symbol by pronouncing its mantra 3 times.

5 Initiations
Opening the Reiki channel and passing on the symbols

Before any initiation
1. The teacher systematically observes the previous steps:
   - **Master preparation.**
   - **Site preparation.**

2. The student sits on a stool (or any backless seat) in the Gasshô pose. Legs uncrossed, feet firmly planted on the floor, eyes closed until the end.

If we have several students to initiate, we observe the two preparations only once per initiation day. As we know, the same initiations are carried out several times for the same degree. They are spread over a period of one to two days or more, depending on the circumstances. You will need to repeat these preparations every day until you have completed the entire initiation process.

It can be very beneficial to recite a mantra or a positive statement indicating our intention. The mantra should be written beforehand. On this occasion, we invite benevolent spiritual beings to actively participate in these initiations.

This statement or mantra could be, for instance:

"I ask and thank my creator (the One...), my spiritual guides (with their names if you are absolutely certain of who they are), the spiritual guides of Mr/Mrs xxxx xxxx (the student's first and surname), the ascended masters, the archangels and all the luminous, benevolent and protective entities who agree to assist me and protect Mr/Mrs xxxx's Level 1 (or any other level) Usui Reiki initiation.
I would like to thank you all and extend my sincere gratitude.
So be it, so be it."

Of course, you can change this mantra to best suit your spiritual affiliations (Gods, Source, etc...). But do not invoke an entity/being whose name could be a source of ambiguity. Do not call upon a deceased loved one. We must imperatively connect to the Source (the One...) by asking for the assistance of luminous entities. Be as clear and simple as possible.

5.1 Level 1 initiation

1. You have observed the preparations for the Master and the location. The student is in place.

2. Gasshô pose (we can recite our mantra now, or before).

The student has their back to you. You stand about three feet away.

3. Let us place our hands on the student's shoulders for a few moments. This gesture has no other purpose than to relax them a little and indicate that the process is beginning. First-level students are sometimes a little stressed for their first initiation.

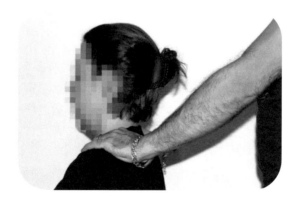

4. Let us trace a **SF** over the entire back, starting at the top of the head (+ SF mantra 3 times).

5. Let us place our hands on the top of the student's head for a moment to establish contact and stimulate their crown chakra.

6. We proceed to the Violet Breath (see Violet Breath chapter).

From then on, the Hui Yin will remain contracted until the end of the initiation.

7. With our dominant hand, we trace an Usui DKM over their head (+ its mantra 3 times). Visualize it entering the top of the head and going down to the base of the skull. You need to "follow" the symbol through with your hand.

The CKR symbol is deliberately left out.

8. With our dominant hand, we trace a SHK over their head (+ SHK mantra 3 times). Visualize it entering the top of the head and going down to the base of the skull. Let us "follow" the symbol through with our hand.

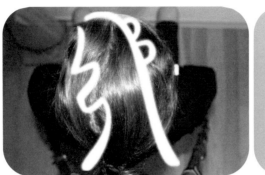 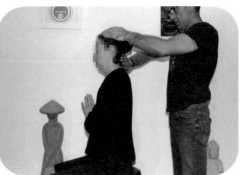

9. With our dominant hand, we trace a HSZSN over their head (+ HSZSN mantra 3 times). Visualize it entering the top of the head and going down to the base of the skull. Let us "follow" the symbol through with our hand.

 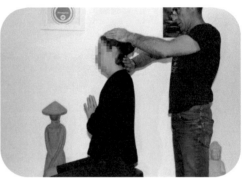

10. We lean forward to take the student's hands and bring them to the top of the head. The student's hands are still clasped together. We support them with our <u>non-dominant</u> hand. Then, with our dominant hand, we trace a CKR over the fingers (+ CKR mantra 3 times). Visualize the symbol entering the hands, the top of the head, and going down to the base of the skull. Let us "follow" the symbol through with our hand.

11. We place their hands back on the heart chakra.

12. We take their hands and open them, palms up. We support the hands with our non-dominant hand.

13. Let us trace a CKR in front of their third eye with our dominant hand (+ corresponding mantra 3 times) and visualize the symbol entering the center of the head and reaching the pineal gland (the third eye is the pineal gland).

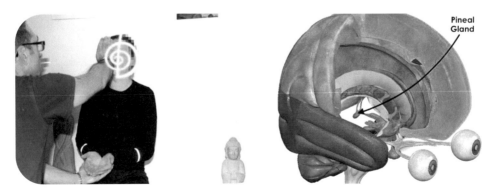

Pineal Gland

14. Let us trace a CKR over their still-open hands with our dominant hand, and visualize the symbol entering their hands. Activate the symbol by uttering its mantra while gently tapping their hands 3 times.

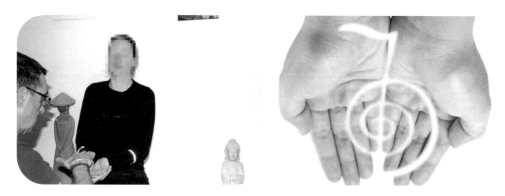

15. Let us close their hands and guide them back to a Gasshô pose.

16. Let us proceed to the Breath of Life (see dedicated chapter).
    Reminder: We trace a CKR while forming a sort of squashed "W" shape with our breath. We need to control our breath and make it last the whole Breath of Life gesture.

Top of the head			3		
Hands	1				5
Solar plexus		2		4	

Reminder: The Hui Yin is still contracted.

17. We place our hands on their shoulders, while visualizing a red sphere of light at the base of their spine, as if we were seeing it through the body and from above.

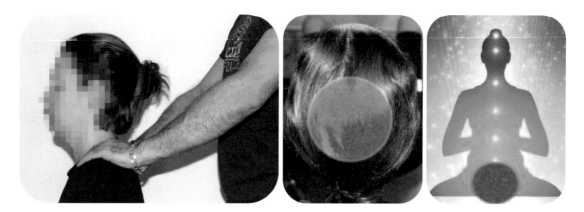

18. We inwardly state the following mantra 3 times, intending it to be received and accepted by the student's unconscious (i.e. their soul): ***"You are a Level 1 Reiki practitioner, with love, trust and success, by the love of the Source."***

19. We place our thumbs together at the base of the person's skull, in the hollow of the neck, and state inwardly, ***"I seal this process with love and divine grace."***

20. We visualize, at the base of their skull, a door that closes and seals itself forever. Then we trace a CHK on it to "lock" the door.

21. We put our hands back on their shoulders, letting feelings of kindness and respect wash over us.

22. Standing about three feet away from the person, we position our hands at hip level, palms facing the student. We inhale deeply, then exhale gently, as if we were blowing a cloud of pure energy around the student. We release the **Hui Yin**. Thus, the energy accumulated throughout the initiation is released from the Hui Yin and washes over the student.

23. We end with a discreet cutting gesture (Kenyo Ku, for instance). Then, we release the person by saying something along the lines of: "Feel free to open your eyes whenever you like". We then show our gratitude with a respectful Gasshô pose (the position the student has been holding since the beginning of the initiation).

If this is the last person we are initiating today, then we gratefully thank all the beings present and all the energetic entities invited.

Steps	The student	Sequence	What we do	Details
1 Preparation	Student in Gasshô pose	1	Preparation	Master/location
		2	Gasshô	Our mantra
2 Behind the student	Their shoulders	3	Laying our hands	
	Top of their head	4	SF	Head & back
		5	Laying our hands	
		6	Violet Breath	Head & Neck
		7	DKM	Head & Neck
		8	SHK	Head & Neck
		9	HSZSN	Head & Neck
	Their hands on their head	10	CKR	Head & Neck
	Their hands on their heart	11	Following the symbol through	
3 In front of the student	Their open hands	12	Following the symbol through	
		13	CKR	Their third eye
		14	CKR	Their hands
		15	Putting them in Gasshô	Guiding their hands
	Their hands in Gasshô	16	Breath of Life	Hui Yin still contracted
4 Behind the student	Their shoulders	17	Laying our hands	Red sphere
		18	Mantra	"You are a practitioner..."
	The hollow of their neck	19	Our thumbs joined	"I seal..."
		20	CKR	The door closes
	Their shoulders	21	Laying our hands	Feel bliss
5 In front of the student	Around them	29	Our hands on our hips	Energy cloud + Hui Yin
		23	Cutting gesture + Gasshô	The student can open their eyes

1
Master and location correctly prepared, student in place.

2

3

4

5

6

7

8

9

10

11

12

13

14

15

16

Breath of Life

Top of the head			3		
Hands	1				5
Solar plexus		2		4	

17

18

"You are a Level 1 Reiki practitioner, with love, trust and success, by the love of the Source."

19

20

21

22

23

We run this initiation process four times over a period of two days, ideally waiting at least two hours between each initiation. In practice, one initiation each morning and one each afternoon (over the two days period) is a perfect pace.

Keep in mind that Level 1 is a big step: there is a lot to say, a lot to absorb and a lot to do for our students.

Do not hesitate to have them work in pairs and share their experience. Beginners will have lots of questions. Also bear in mind that some people may be a little stressed, and that there is no such thing as a bad question.

Time needed between Level 1 & Level 2 initiations: three months.

5.2 Level 2 Initiation

1. You have observed the preparations for the Master and the location. The student is in place.

2. Gasshô (we can recite our mantra now, or before).

The student has their back to you. You stand about three feet away.

3. Let us place our hands on the student's shoulders for a few moments. This gesture has no other purpose than to relax them a little and indicate that the process is beginning.

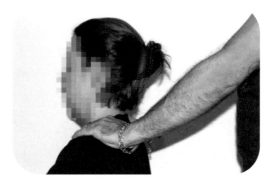

4. Let us trace a SF over the entire back, starting at the top of the head (+ SF mantra 3 times).

5. Let us place our hands on the top of the student's head for a moment to establish contact and stimulate their crown chakra.

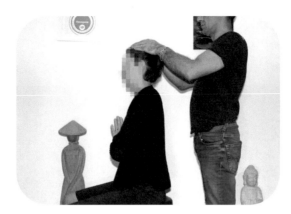

6. We proceed to the Violet Breath (see Violet Breath chapter)

From then on, the Hui Yin will remain contracted until the end of the initiation.

7. With our dominant hand, we trace an Usui DKM over their head (+ its mantra 3 times). Visualize it entering the top of the head and going down to the base of the skull. You need to "follow" the symbol through with your hand.

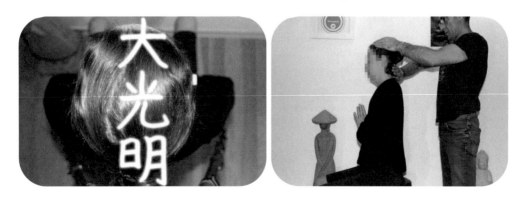

8. We lean forward to take the student's hands and bring them to the top of their head. Their hands are still clasped. We support them with our non-dominant hand. Then, with our dominant hand, we trace a SKSK over their fingers (+ corresponding mantra 3 times). Visualize the symbol entering their hands, the top of their head, and going down to the base of their skull. Let us "follow" the symbol through with our hand.

9. We trace a CKR over their fingers (+ corresponding mantra 3 times). Visualize the symbol entering their hands, the top of their head, and going down to the base of their skull. Let us "follow" the symbol through with our hand.

10. We trace a SHK over their fingers (+ corresponding mantra 3 times). Visualize the symbol entering their hands, the top of their head, and going down to the base of their skull. Let us "follow" the symbol through with our hand.

11. We trace a HSZSN over their fingers (+ corresponding mantra 3 times). Visualize the symbol entering their hands, the top of their head, and going down to the base of their skull. Let us "follow" the symbol through with our hand.

12. We place their hands back on the heart chakra.

5.2.3 Step 3 - In front of the student: Hands, body, consciousness

13. We take their hands and open them, palms up. We support the hands with our non-dominant hand.

14. Let us trace a SKSK in front of their third eye with our dominant hand (+ corresponding mantra 3 times) and visualize the symbol entering the center of the head and reaching the pineal gland (the third eye is the pineal gland). We need to adjust the size of the symbols to match the person's forehead. The symbols are only enlarged here for better clarity.

15. Let us trace a CKR in front of their third eye with our dominant hand (+ corresponding mantra 3 times) and visualize the symbol entering the head and reaching its center (i.e. the pineal gland).

16. Let us trace a SHK in front of their third eye with our dominant hand (+ corresponding mantra 3 times) and visualize the symbol entering the head and reaching its center (i.e. the pineal gland).

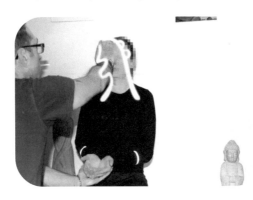

17. Let us trace a HSZSN in front of their third eye with our dominant hand (+ corresponding mantra 3 times) and visualize the symbol entering the head and reaching its center (i.e. the pineal gland).

18. Let us trace a SKSK over their still-open hands with our dominant hand, and visualize the symbol entering their hands. Activate the symbol by uttering its mantra while gently tapping their hands 3 times.

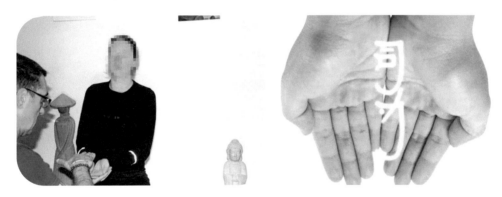

19. Trace a CKR over their hands and visualize the symbol entering their hands. Activate the symbol by uttering its mantra while gently tapping their hands 3 times.

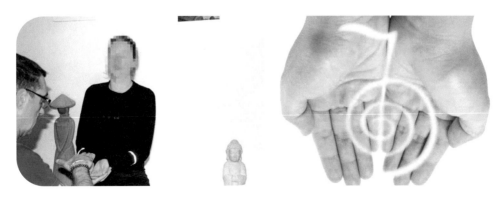

20. Trace a SHK over their hands and visualize the symbol entering their hands. Activate the symbol by uttering its mantra while gently tapping their hands 3 times.

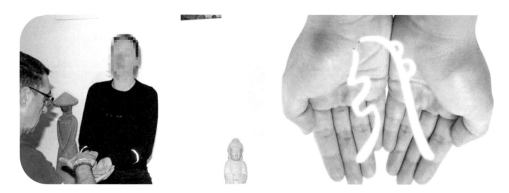

21. Trace a HSZSN over their hands and visualize the symbol entering their hands. Activate the symbol by uttering its mantra while gently tapping their hands 3 times.

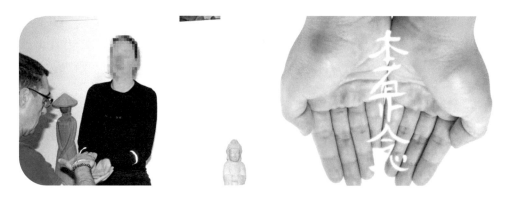

22. Let us close their hands and guide them back to a Gasshô pose.

23. Let proceed to the Breath of Life (see dedicated chapter). *Reminder: We trace a CKR while forming a sort of squashed "W" shape with our breath. We need to control our breath and make it last the whole Breath of Life gesture.*

Top of the head			3		
Hands	1				5
Solar plexus		2		4	

Reminder: The Hui Yin is still contracted.

24. We place our hands on their shoulders, while visualizing a red sphere of light at the base of their spine, as if we were seeing it through the body and from above.

25. We inwardly state the following mantra 3 times, intending it to be received and accepted by the student's unconscious (i.e. their soul): ***"You are a Level 2 Reiki practitioner, with love, trust and success, by the love of the Source."***

26. We place our thumbs together at the base of the person's skull, in the hollow of the neck, and state inwardly, ***"I seal this process with love and divine grace."***

27. We visualize, at the base of their skull, a door that closes and seals itself forever. Then we trace a CHK on it to "lock" the door.

28. We put our hands back on their shoulders, letting feelings of kindness and respect wash over us.

5.2.5   Step 5 - In front of the pupil: Transmitting accumulated energy

29. Standing about three feet away from the person, we position our hands at hip level, palms facing the student. We inhale deeply, then exhale gently, as if we were blowing a cloud of pure energy around the student. We release the **Hui Yin**. Thus, the energy accumulated throughout the initiation is released from the Hui Yin and washes over the student.

30. We end with a discreet cutting gesture (Kenyo Ku, for instance). Then, we release the person by saying something along the lines of: "Feel free to open your eyes whenever you like". We then show our gratitude with a respectful Gasshô pose (the position the student has been holding since the beginning of the initiation).

5.2.6   Step 6 - Last initiation of the day

If this is the last person we are initiating today, then we gratefully thank all the beings present and all the energetic entities invited.

Steps	The student	Sequence	What we do	Details
1 Preparation	Student in Gasshô pose	1	Preparation	Master/location
		2	Gasshô	Our mantra
2 Behind the student	Their shoulders	3	Laying our hands	
	Top of their head	4	SF	Head & back
		5	Laying our hands	Contact
		6	Violet Breath	Head & Neck
		7	DKM	Head & Neck
	Their hands on their head	8	SKSK	Head & Neck
		9	CKR	Head & Neck
		10	SHK	Head & Neck
		11	HSZSN	Head & Neck
	Their hands on their heart	12	Following the symbol through	
3 In front of the student	Their open hands	13	Following the symbol through	
		14	SKSK	Their third eye
		15	CKR	Their third eye
		16	SHK	Their third eye
		17	HSZSN	Their third eye
		18	SKSK	Their hands
		19	CKR	Their hands
		20	SHK	Their hands
		21	HSZSN	Their hands
		22	Putting them in Gasshô	Guiding their hands
	Their hands in Gasshô	23	Breath of Life	Hui Yin still contracted
4 Behind the student	Their shoulders	24	Laying our hands	Red sphere
		25	Mantra	"You are a practitioner..."
	The hollow of their neck	26	Our thumbs joined	"I seal..."
		27	CKR	The door closes
	Their shoulders	28	Laying our hands	Feel bliss
5 In front of the student	Around them	29	Our hands on our hips	Energy cloud + Hui Yin
		30	Cutting gesture + Gasshô	The student can open their eyes

1
Master and location correctly prepared, student in place.

2

3

4

5

6

7

8

9

10

11

12

13

14

15

16

17

18

19

20

21

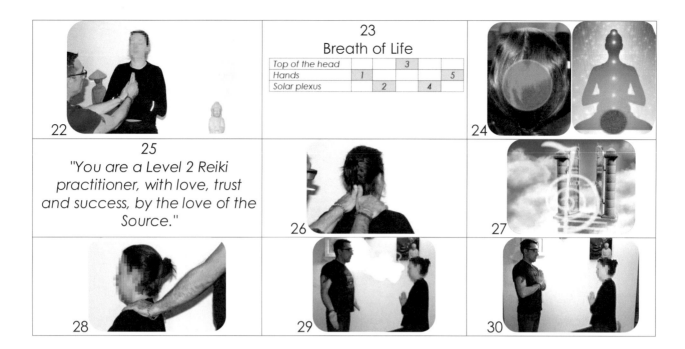

23
Breath of Life

	1	2	3	4	5
Top of the head			3		
Hands	1				5
Solar plexus		2		4	

25
"You are a Level 2 Reiki practitioner, with love, trust and success, by the love of the Source."

5.2.8 Level 2 initiation in practice

We run this initiation process three times over a period of a day and a half, ideally waiting at least two hours between each initiation. In practice, I personally do one initiation on the first day and two on the second day: one mid-morning and one mid-afternoon.

Level 2 is a big step, but it is less intense than Level 1. The main difficulty lies in learning the symbols without distorting them too much. Ask your students to practice, on paper and in the air (while standing behind them).

Do not hesitate to get them to work in pairs and share their feelings.

Time needed between Level 2 & Level 3 initiations: nine months.

5.3   Level 3 Initiation

$\triangle$ **At this stage, it is a good idea to do the heart and feet initiation before this one.**

---

1. You have observed the preparations for the Master and the location. The student is in place.
2. Gasshô pose (we can recite our mantra now, or before).

3. Let us place our hands on the student's shoulders for a few moments. This gesture has no other purpose than to indicate that the process is beginning.

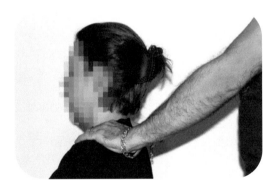

4. Let us trace a SF over the entire back, starting at the top of the head (+ SF mantra 3 times).

5. Let us place our hands on the top of their head for a moment to establish contact and stimulate their crown chakra.

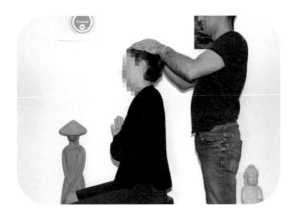

6. We proceed to the Violet Breath (see Violet Breath chapter)

From then on, the Hui Yin will remain contracted until the end of the initiation.

7. We lean forward to take the student's hands and bring them to the top of their head. Their hands are still clasped. We support them with our non-dominant hand. Then, with our dominant hand, we trace a DKM over their fingers (+ 3 mantras). Visualize it entering their hands, the top of their head, and going down to the base of their skull. Let us "follow" the symbol through with our hand.

8. We trace a SKSK over their fingers (+ 3 mantras). Visualize it entering their hands, the top of their head, and going down to the base of their skull. Let us "follow" the symbol through with our hand.

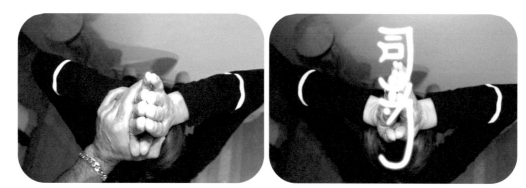

9. We trace a CKR over their fingers (+ 3 mantras). Visualize it entering their hands, the top of their head, and going down to the base of their skull. Let us "follow" the symbol through with our hand.

10. We trace a SHK over their fingers (+ 3 mantras). Visualize it entering their hands, the top of their head, and going down to the base of their skull. We "follow" the symbol through with our hand.

11. We trace a HSZSN over their fingers (+ 3 mantras). Visualize it entering their hands, the top of their head, and going down to the base of their skull. We "follow" the symbol through with our hand.

12. We place their hands back on the heart chakra.

5.3.3 Step 3 - In front of the student: Hands, body, consciousness

13. We take their hands and open them, palms up. We support the hands with our non-dominant hand.

14. Let us trace a SKSK in front of their third eye with our dominant hand (+ corresponding mantra 3 times) and visualize the symbol entering the center of the head and reaching the pineal gland (the third eye is the pineal gland). We need to adjust the size of the symbols to match the person's forehead. The symbols are only enlarged here for better clarity.

15. Let us trace a SKSK in front of their third eye with our dominant hand (+ corresponding mantra 3 times) and visualize the symbol entering the center of the head and reaching the pineal gland. We need to adjust the size of the symbols to match the person's forehead. The symbols are only enlarged here for better clarity.

16. Let us trace a CKR in front of their third eye with our dominant hand (+ corresponding mantra 3 times) and visualize the symbol entering the center of the head and reaching the pineal gland.

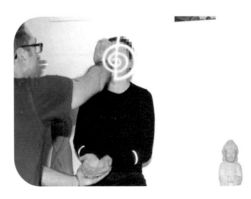

17. Let us trace a SHK in front of their third eye with our dominant hand (+ corresponding mantra 3 times) and visualize the symbol entering the center of the head and reaching the pineal gland.

18. Let us trace a HSZSN in front of their third eye with our dominant hand (+ corresponding mantra 3 times) and visualize the symbol entering the center of the head and reaching the pineal gland.

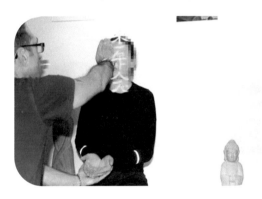

19. Let us trace a DKM over their still-open hands with our dominant hand, and visualize the symbol entering their hands. Activate the symbol by uttering its mantra while gently tapping their hands 3 times.

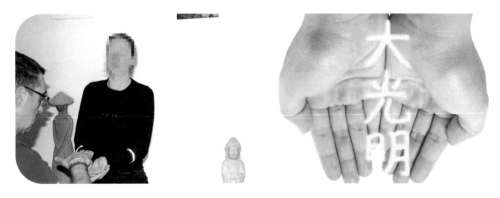

20. Let us trace a SKSK over their still-open hands with our dominant hand, and visualize the symbol entering their hands. Activate the symbol by uttering its mantra while gently tapping their hands 3 times.

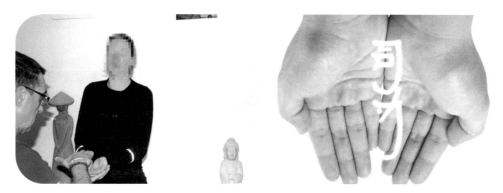

21. Let us trace a CKR over their still-open hands with our dominant hand, and visualize the symbol entering their hands. Activate the symbol by uttering its mantra while gently tapping their hands 3 times.

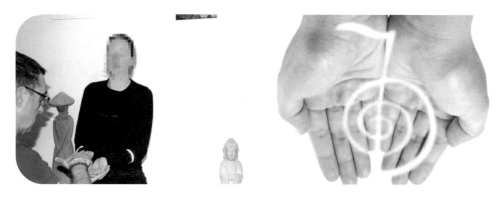

22. Let us trace a SHK over their still-open hands with our dominant hand, and visualize the symbol entering their hands. Activate the symbol by uttering its mantra while gently tapping their hands 3 times.

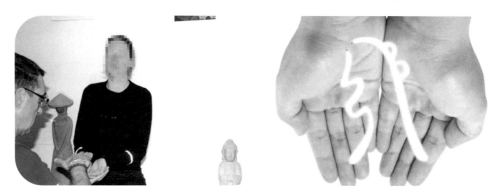

23. Trace HSZSN over their still-open hands with our dominant hand, and visualize the symbol entering their hands. Activate the symbol by uttering its mantra while gently tapping their hands 3 times.

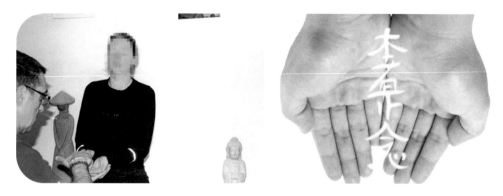

24. Let us close their hands and guide them back to a Gasshô pose

25. Let us proceed to the Breath of Life (see dedicated chapter).
Reminder: We trace a CKR while forming a sort of squashed "W" shape with our breath. We need to control our breath and make it last the whole Breath of Life gesture.

Top of the head			3		
Hands	1				5
Solar plexus		2		4	

Reminder: The Hui Yin is still contracted.

26. We place our hands on their shoulders, while visualizing a red sphere of light at the base of their spine, as if we were seeing it through the body and from above.

27. We inwardly state the following mantra 3 times, intending it to be received and accepted by the student's unconscious (i.e. their soul): **"You are a Level 3 Reiki practitioner, with love, trust and success, by the love of the Source."**

28. We place our thumbs together at the base of the person's skull, in the hollow of the neck, and state inwardly, **"I seal this process with love and divine grace."**

29. We visualize, at the base of their skull, a door that closes and seals itself forever. Then we trace a CHK on it to "lock" the door.

30. We put our hands back on their shoulders, letting feelings of kindness and respect wash over us.

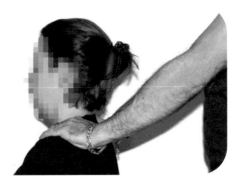

31. Standing about three feet away from the person, we position our hands at hip level, palms facing the student. We inhale deeply, then exhale gently, as if we were blowing a cloud of pure energy around the student. We release the **Hui Yin**. Thus, the energy accumulated throughout the initiation is released from the Hui Yin and washes over the student.

32. We end with a discreet cutting gesture (Kenyo Ku, for instance). Then, we release the person by saying something along the lines of: "Feel free to open your eyes whenever you like". We then show our gratitude with a respectful Gasshô pose (the position the student has been holding since the beginning of the initiation).

If this is the last person we are initiating today, then we gratefully thank all the beings present and all the energetic entities invited.

Steps	The student	Sequence	What we do	Details
1 Preparation	Student in Gasshô pose	1	Preparation	Master/location
		2	Gasshô	Our mantra
2 Behind the student	Their shoulders	3	Laying our hands	
	Top of their head	4	SF	Head & back
		5	Laying our hands	Contact
		6	Violet Breath	Head & Neck
	Their hands on their head	7	DKM	Head & Neck
		8	SKSK	Head & Neck
		9	CKR	Head & Neck
		10	SHK	Head & Neck
		11	HSZSN	Head & Neck
	Their hands on their heart	12	Following the symbol through	
3 In front of the student	Their open hands	13	Following the symbol through	
		14	DKM	Their third eye
		15	SKSK	Their third eye
		16	CKR	Their third eye
		17	SHK	Their third eye
		18	HSZSN	Their third eye
		19	DKM	Their hands
		20	SKSK	Their hands
		21	CKR	Their hands
		22	SHK	Their hands
		23	HSZSN	Their hands
		24	Putting them in Gasshô	Guiding their hands
	Their hands in Gasshô	25	Breath of Life	Hui Yin still contracted
4 Behind the student	Their shoulders	26	Laying our hands	Red sphere
		27	Mantra	"You are a practitioner..."
	The hollow of their neck	28	Our thumbs joined	"I seal..."
	Their shoulders	29	CKR	The door closes
	Their shoulders	30	Laying our hands	Feel bliss
5 In front of the student	Around them	31	Our hands on our hips	Energy cloud + Hui Yin
		32	Cutting gesture + Gasshô	The student can open their eyes

1
Master and location correctly prepared, student in place.

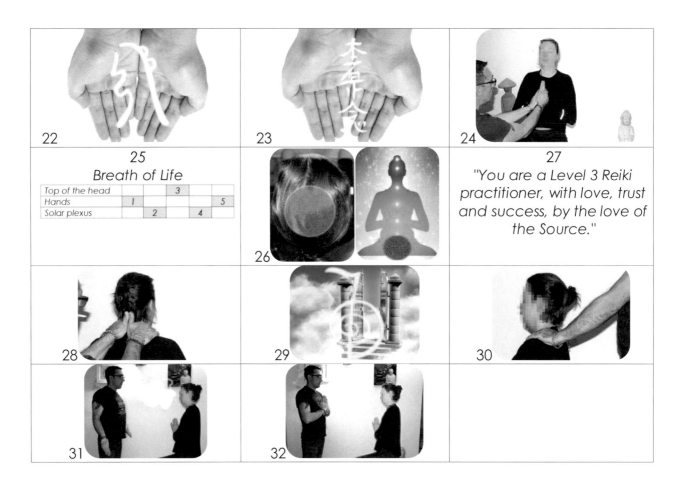

5.3.8 Level 3 initiation in practice

We only do this initiation process once over a period of a day and a half or two days, ideally doing the heart and feet initiation (see following chapters) before the Level 3 initiation. We need to wait two hours between the heart and feet initiation and the Level 3 initiation.

Time needed between Level 3 & Level 4 initiations: six months.

5.4 Level 4 initiation: Reiki Mastery

> $\triangle$ **At this stage, it is a good idea to redo the heart and feet initiation before this one.**

1. You have observed the preparations for the Master and the location. The student is in place. **However, we need to add the TDKM on our hands before the DKM and the CKR.**

2. Gasshô pose (we can recite our mantra now, or before).

3. Let us place our hands on the student's shoulders for a few moments. This gesture has no other purpose than to indicate that the process is beginning.

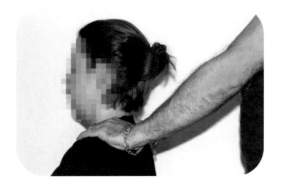

4. Let us trace a SF over the entire back, starting at the top of the head (+ 3 SF mantras).

5. Let us place our hands on the top of the head for a few moments to establish **deep** contact.

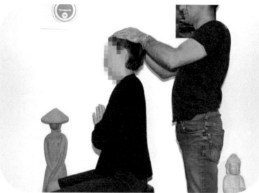

6. We lean forward, take their hands and bring them to the top of their head. We do the Violet Breath on their fingers (see Violet Breath chapter).

We visualize the purple energy (and its symbol) entering the student's fingers and passing through their head. With our dominant hand, we "follow" it to the base of the skull.

From then on, the Hui Yin will remain contracted until the end of the initiation.

7. We trace a TDKM over their fingers (+ 3 mantras). Visualize the symbol entering their hands, the top of their head, and going down to the base of their skull. Let us "follow" the symbol through with our hand.

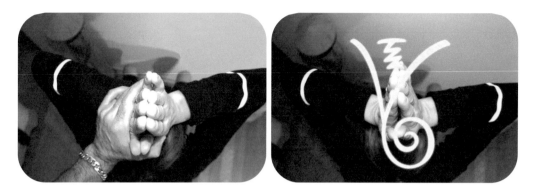

8. We trace a SF over their fingers (+ 3 mantras). Visualize the symbol entering their hands, the top of their head, and going down to the base of their skull. We "follow" the symbol through with our hand.

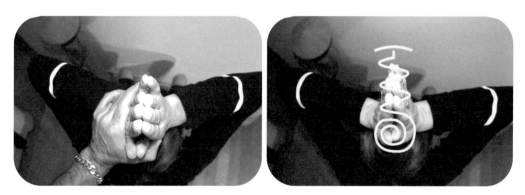

9. We trace a DF over their fingers (+ 3 mantras). Visualize the symbol entering their hands, the top of their head, and going down to the base of their skull. We "follow" the symbol through with our hand.

10. We trace a CKS over their fingers (+ 3 mantras). Visualize the symbol entering their hands, the top of their head, and going down to the base of their skull. We "follow" the symbol through with our hand.

11. We trace a DKM over their fingers (+ 3 mantras). Visualize the symbol entering their hands, the top of their head, and going down to the base of their skull. We "follow" the symbol through with our hand.

12. We trace a SKSK over their fingers (+ 3 mantras). Visualize the symbol entering their hands, the top of their head, and going down to the base of their skull. We "follow" the symbol through with our hand.

13. We trace a CKR over their fingers (+ 3 mantras). Visualize the symbol entering their hands, the top of their head, and going down to the base of their skull. We "follow" the symbol through with our hand.

14. We trace a SHK over their fingers (+ 3 mantras). Visualize the symbol entering their hands, the top of their head, and going down to the base of their skull. We "follow" the symbol through with our hand.

15. We trace a HSZSN over their fingers (+ 3 mantras). Visualize the symbol entering their hands, the top of their head, and going down to the base of their skull. We "follow" the symbol through with our hand.

 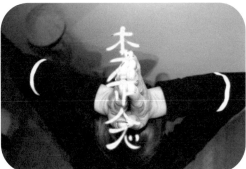

16. We place their hands back on the heart chakra.

17. We take their hands and open them, palms up. We support them with our non-dominant hand.

18. Let us trace a TDKM in front of their third eye with our dominant hand (+ corresponding mantra 3 times) and visualize the symbol entering the center of the head and reaching the pineal gland (the third eye is the pineal gland). We need to adjust the size of the symbols to match the person's forehead. The symbols are only enlarged here for better clarity.

19. Let us trace a SF in front of its third eye with our dominant hand (+ corresponding mantra 3 times) and visualize the symbol entering the center of the head and reaching the pineal gland.

20. Let us trace a DF in front of their third eye with our dominant hand (+ corresponding mantra 3 times) and visualize the symbol entering the center of the head and reaching the pineal gland.

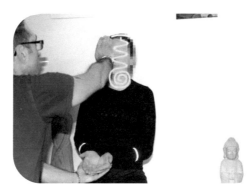

21. Let us trace a CKS in front of their third eye with our dominant hand (+ corresponding mantra 3 times) and visualize the symbol entering the center of the head to the pineal gland.

22. Let us trace a DKM in front of their third eye with our dominant hand (+ corresponding mantra 3 times) and visualize the symbol entering the center of the head and the pineal gland.

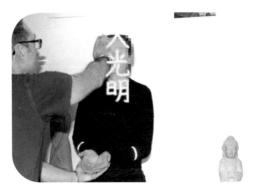

23. Let us trace a SKSK in front of their third eye with our dominant hand (+ corresponding mantra 3 times) and visualize the symbol entering the center of the head and reaching the pineal gland. We need to adjust the size of the symbols to match the person's forehead. The symbols are only enlarged here for better clarity.

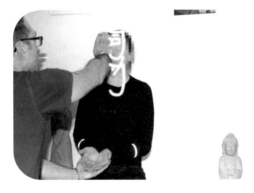

24. Let us trace a CKR in front of their third eye with our dominant hand (+ corresponding mantra 3 times) and visualize the symbol entering the center of the head and the pineal gland.

25. Let us trace a SHK in front of their third eye with our dominant hand (+ corresponding mantra 3 times) and visualize the symbol entering the center of the head and reaching the pineal gland.

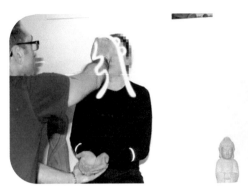

26. Let us trace a HSZSN in front of their third eye with our dominant hand (+ corresponding mantra 3 times) and visualize the symbol entering the center of the head and reaching the pineal gland.

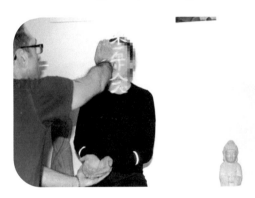

27. Let us trace a TDKM over their still-open hands with our dominant hand, and visualize the symbol entering their hands. Activate the symbol by uttering its mantra while gently tapping their hands 3 times.

28. Let us trace a SF over their still-open hands with our dominant hand, and visualize the symbol entering their hands. Activate the symbol by uttering its mantra while gently tapping their hands 3 times.

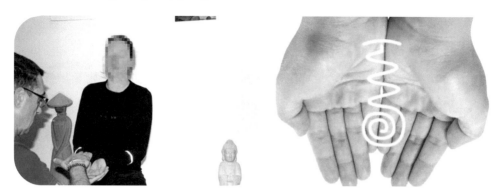

29. Let us trace a DF over their still-open hands with our dominant hand, and visualize the symbol entering their hands. Activate the symbol by uttering its mantra while gently tapping their hands 3 times.

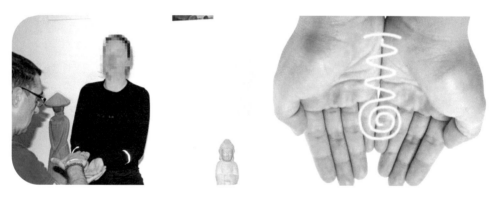

30. Let us trace a CKS over their still-open hands with our dominant hand, and visualize the symbol entering their hands. Activate the symbol by uttering its mantra while gently tapping their hands 3 times.

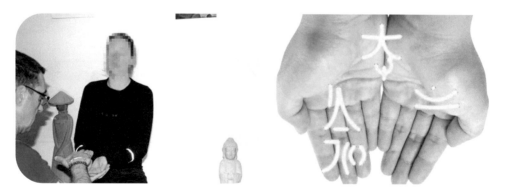

31. Let us trace a DKM over their still-open hands with our dominant hand, and visualize the symbol entering their hands. Activate the symbol by uttering its mantra while gently tapping their hands 3 times.

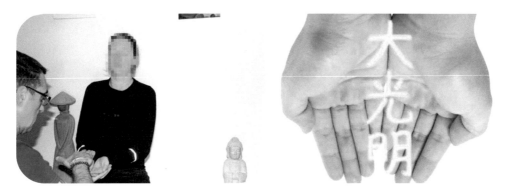

32. Let us trace a SKSK over their still-open hands with our dominant hand, and visualize the symbol entering their hands. Activate the symbol by uttering its mantra while gently tapping their hands 3 times.

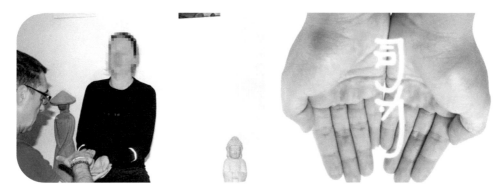

33. Let us trace a CKR over their still-open hands with our dominant hand, and visualize the symbol entering their hands. Activate the symbol by uttering its mantra while gently tapping their hands 3 times.

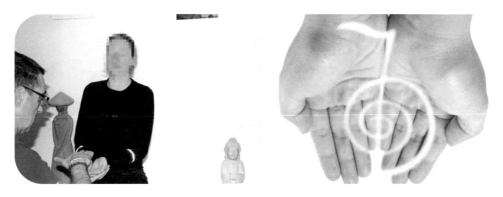

34. Let us trace a SHK over their still-open hands with our dominant hand, and visualize the symbol entering their hands. Activate the symbol by uttering its mantra while gently tapping their hands 3 times.

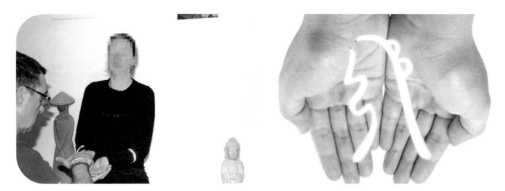

35. Trace HSZSN over their still-open hands with our dominant hand, and visualize the symbol entering their hands. Activate the symbol by uttering its mantra while gently tapping their hands 3 times.

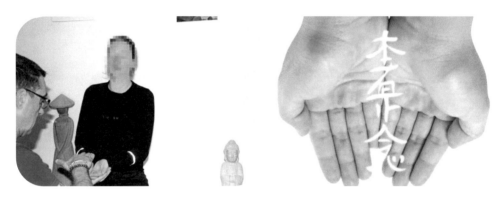

36. Let us close their hands and guide them back to a Gasshô pose.

37. Let us proceed to the Breath of Life (see dedicated chapter).
    Reminder: We trace a CKR while forming a sort of squashed "W" shape with our breath. We need to control our breath and make it last the whole Breath of Life gesture.

Top of the head			*3*		
Hands	*1*				*5*
Solar plexus		*2*		*4*	

Reminder: The Hui Yin is still contracted.

38. We place our hands on their shoulders while visualizing a red sphere of light at the base of their spine, as if we were seeing it through the body and from above.

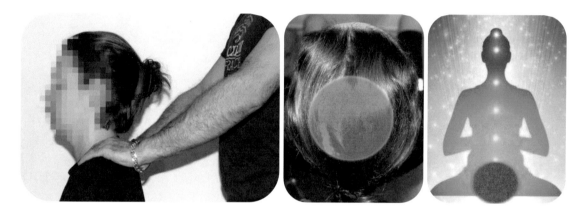

39. We inwardly state the following mantra 3 times, intending it to be received and accepted by the student's unconscious (i.e. their soul): ***"You are a Reiki Master, with love, trust and success, by the love of the Source."***

40. We place our thumbs together at the base of the person's skull, in the hollow of the neck, and state inwardly, ***"I seal this process with love and divine grace."***

41. We visualize, at the base of their skull, a door that closes and seals itself forever. Then we trace a CHK on it to "lock" the door.

42. We put our hands back on their shoulders, letting feelings of kindness and respect wash over us.

5.4.5 Step 5 - In front of the pupil: Transmitting accumulated energy

43. Standing about three feet away from the person, we position our hands at hip level, palms facing the student. We inhale deeply, then exhale gently, as if we were blowing a cloud of pure energy around the student. We release the **Hui Yin**. Thus, the energy accumulated throughout the initiation is released from the Hui Yin and washes over the student.

44. We end with a discreet cutting gesture (Kenyo Ku, for instance). Then, we release the person by saying something along the lines of: "Feel free to open your eyes whenever you like". We then show our gratitude with a respectful Gasshô pose.

5.4.6 Step 6 - Last initiation of the day

If this is the last person we are initiating today, then we gratefully thank all the beings present and all the energetic entities invited.

Steps	The student	Seq.	What we do	Details
1 Preparation	Student in Gasshô pose	1	Preparation + **Adding TDKM**	Master/location
		2	Gasshô	Our mantra
2 Behind the student	Their shoulders	3	Laying our hands	
	Top of their head	4	SF	Head & back
		5	Laying our hands	Contact
	Their hands on their head	6	Violet Breath	Fingers/neck
		7	TDKM	Fingers/neck
		8	SF	Fingers/neck
		9	DF	Fingers/neck
		10	CKS	Fingers/neck
		11	DKM	Fingers/neck
		12	SKSK	Fingers/neck
		13	CKR	Fingers/neck
		14	SHK	Fingers/neck
		15	HSZSN	Fingers/neck
	Their hands on their heart	16	Following the symbol through	
3 In front of the student	Their open hands	17		
		18	TDKM	Their third eye
		19	SF	Their third eye
		20	DF	Their third eye
		21	CKS	Their third eye
		22	DKM	Their third eye
		23	SKSK	Their third eye
		24	CKR	Their third eye
		25	SHK	Their third eye
		26	HSZSN	Their third eye
		27	TDKM	Their hands
		28	SF	Their hands
		29	DF	Their hands
		30	CKS	Their hands
		31	DKM	Their hands
		32	SKSK	Their hands
		33	CKR	Their hands
		34	SHK	Their hands
		35	HSZSN	Their hands
		36	Putting them in Gasshô	Guiding them
	Their hands in Gasshô	37	Breath of Life	Hui Yin still contracted
4 Behind the student	Their shoulders	38	Laying our hands	Red sphere
		39	Mantra	"You are a Master..."
	The hollow of their neck	40	Our thumbs joined	"I seal..."
	Their shoulders	41	CKR	The door closes
	Their shoulders	42	Laying our hands	Feel bliss
5 In front of the student	Around them	43	Our hands on our hips	Energy cloud + Hui Yin
		44	Cutting gesture + Gasshô	The student can open their eyes

1
Master and location correctly prepared, student in place.

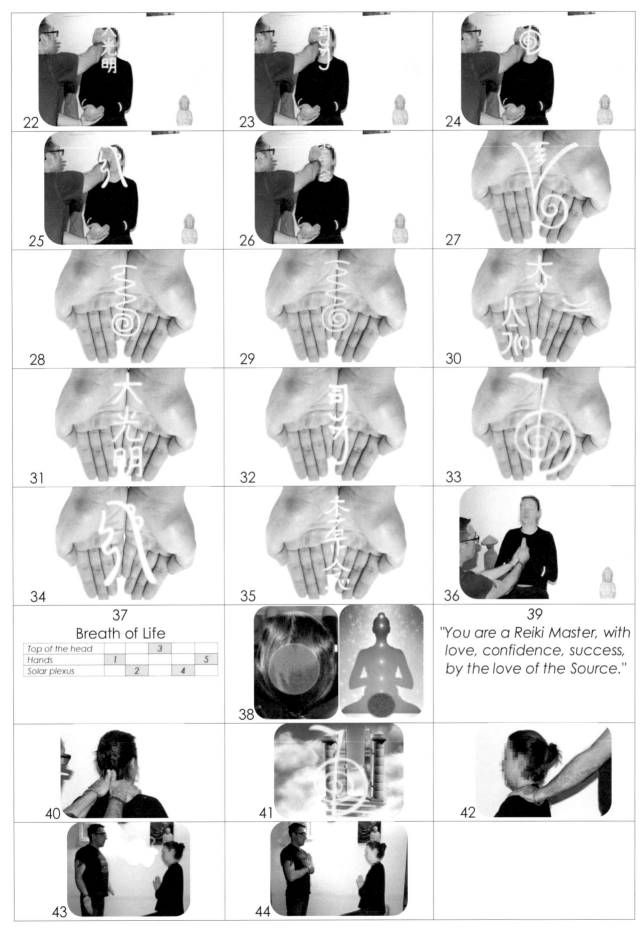

22

23

24

25

26

27

28

29

30

31

32

33

34

35

36

37
Breath of Life

	1	2	3	4	5
Top of the head			3		
Hands	1				5
Solar plexus		2		4	

38

39
"You are a Reiki Master, with love, confidence, success, by the love of the Source."

40

41

42

43

44

We only do this initiation process once over a period of a day and a half or two days, ideally doing the heart and feet initiation (see next chapter) before the Level 4 initiation, so as to make an energetic preparation. We need to wait two hours between the heart and feet initiation and the Level 4 initiation.

5.5   Initiation of the heart and feet

1. You have observed the preparations for the Master and the location. The student is in place.
   Some significant differences in this initiation:
   A) During our mantra, our statement should mention that this is **an initiation of the heart symbol and an initiation of the feet.**
   B) We trace the following 7 symbols around the room with their corresponding mantras (3 times) in this order:
      a. TDKM
      b. SF
      c. SKSK
      d. DKM
      e. CKR
      f. SHK
      g. HSZSN

2. Gasshô pose (we can recite our mantra now, or before).

3. Let us place our hands on the student's shoulders for a few moments. This gesture indicates that the process is beginning.

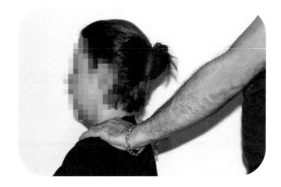

4. Let us trace a SF over the entire back, starting at the top of the head (+ 3 SF mantras).

5. Let us place our hands on the top of the head for a few moments to establish **deep** contact.

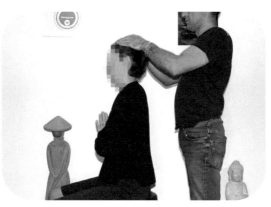

6. We proceed to the Violet Breath (see Violet Breath chapter)

From then on, the Hui Yin will remain contracted until the end of the initiation.

7. With our dominant hand, we trace an Usui DKM over their head (+ 3 DKM mantras). Visualize the symbol entering the top of the head and going down to the base of the skull. Let us "follow" the symbol through with our hand.

8. We lean forward to take the student's hands and bring them to the top of their head. Their hands are still clasped. We support them with our non-dominant hand. Then, with our dominant hand, we trace a SKSK over their fingers (+ 3 SKSK mantras). Visualize the symbol entering their hands, the top of their head, and going down to the base of their skull. Let us "follow" the symbol through with our hand.

9. We place their hands back on the heart chakra.

10. We take their hands and open them, palms up. We support them with our non-dominant hand.

11. Let us trace a SKSK in front of their third eye with our dominant hand (+ corresponding mantra 3 times) and visualize the symbol entering the center of the head and reaching the pineal gland (the third eye is the pineal gland). We need to adjust the size of the symbols to match the person's forehead. The symbols are only enlarged here for better clarity.

12. Let us trace a SKSK in front of their heart chakra with our dominant hand (+ corresponding mantra 3 times) and visualize the symbol entering the heart.

13. Let us trace a SKSK over their still-open hands with our dominant hand, and visualize the symbol entering their hands. Activate the symbol by uttering its mantra while gently tapping their hands 3 times.

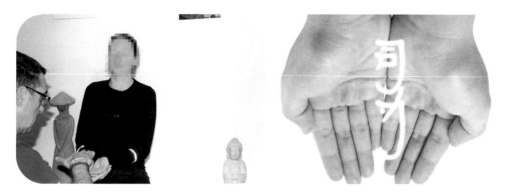

14. Let us close their hands and guide them back to a Gasshô pose.

15. Let us proceed to the Breath of Life (see dedicated chapter).
    Reminder: We trace a CKR while forming a sort of squashed "W" shape with our breath. We need to control our breath and make it last the whole Breath of Life gesture.

Top of the head			3		
Hands	1				5
Solar plexus		2		4	

Reminder: The Hui Yin is still contracted.

16. Let us kneel down and place our hands on the student's feet. Trace a TDKM (+ corresponding mantra 3 times) in the space between the two feet. Visualize the energy of the symbol uniting the feet like a bridge.

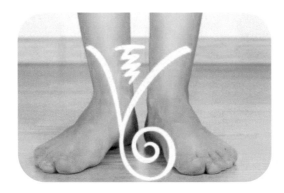

17. Let us choose one foot or the other.

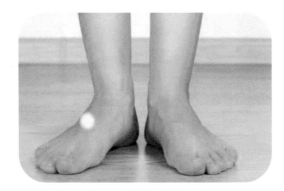

18. Let us trace an Usui DKM now, visualizing the energy of the symbol penetrating this foot while activating it (by uttering the 3 mantras).

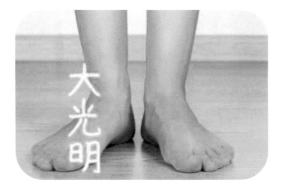

19. Let us trace a CKR, visualizing the energy of the symbol penetrating this foot while activating it (by uttering the 3 mantras).

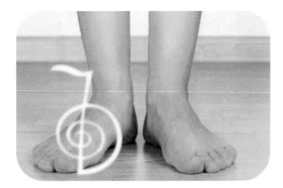

20. Let us trace a SHK, visualizing the energy of the symbol penetrating this foot while activating it (by uttering the 3 mantras).

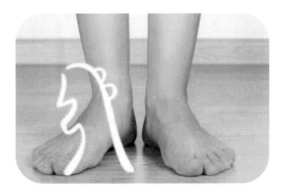

21. Let us trace a HSZSN, visualizing the energy of the symbol penetrating this foot while activating it (by uttering the 3 mantras).

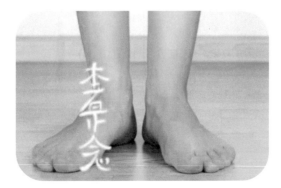

22. Let us repeat this process from step 17 with the other foot.

23. We remove our hands.

24. Let us proceed to the Breath of Life on the feet (see the Breath of Life chapter).
   Reminder: We trace a CKR while blowing on one foot and then the other, at a distance of a few inches.

Foot 1	1
Foot 2	2

We then stand up, our **Hui Yin still contracted.**

5.5.4 Step 4 - Behind the student: They become a Reiki practitioner

25. We place our hands on their shoulders, while visualizing a red sphere of light at the base of their spine, as if we were seeing it through the body and from above.

26. We inwardly state the following mantra 3 times, intending it to be received and accepted by the student's unconscious (i.e. their soul): *"You are a Reiki practitioner/Master, with love, trust and success, by the love of the Source."*

27. We place our thumbs together at the base of the person's skull, in the hollow of the neck, and state inwardly, *"I seal this process with love and divine grace."*

28. We visualize, at the base of their skull, a door that closes and seals itself forever. Then we trace a CHK on it to "lock" the door.

29. We put our hands back on their shoulders, letting feelings of kindness and respect wash over us.

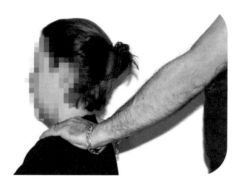

5.5.5 Step 5 - In front of the pupil: Transmitting accumulated energy

30. Standing about three feet away from the person, we position our hands at hip level, palms facing the student. We inhale deeply, then exhale gently, as if we were blowing a cloud of pure energy around the student. We release the **Hui Yin**. Thus, the energy accumulated throughout the initiation is released from the Hui Yin and washes over the student.

6   Healing attunement

Healing attunement has two advantages. Non only is it an extremely powerful and intense Reiki treatment, it is also equivalent to the most beautiful of prayers, whatever the religious beliefs of the recipient and the practitioner.

It is recommended in cases where the recipient is facing a major milestone in their life (a certification exam, a medical operation, before a Reiki treatment which, as we already know, will take at least four sessions, etc.).

This treatment is so important and so intense that a number of symptomatic disorders can occur afterwards. This is why it can be important to warn the recipient of them: nausea, digestive disturbances, excessive sweating... or any other healing crisis. This is something we have already covered in previous courses.

Anyone can receive this healing attunement: Reiki initiate or not. Technically, it is not an initiation since we do not work on their hands. But the recipient does receive a huge amount of energy in a very short space of time. It is a very intense and effective treatment.

6.1   Step 1 - Preparations

> **1.   You have observed the preparations for the Master and the location, the recipient is in place with their hands resting on their knees, eyes closed.**

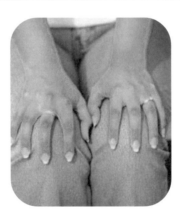

For this preparation in particular: Our mantra should mention that this is a healing attunement rather than an initiation.

2.   Gasshô pose (we can recite our mantra now, or before).

6.2 Step 2 - Behind the recipient

3. Let us trace a SF over the entire back, starting at the top of the head (+ 3 SF mantras).

4. Let us place our hands on the top of the head for a moment to establish energetic contact.

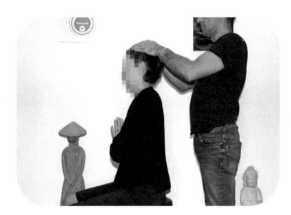

5. We proceed to the Violet Breath (see chapter on the Violet Breath) and lead the purple energy and its symbol to the heart chakra (seen from the student's back).

From then on, the Hui Yin will remain contracted until the end of the exercise.

6. With our dominant hand, we trace an Usui DKM over their head. **Visualize it entering the top of the head, then going down to the heart chakra. You need to "follow" the symbol through with your dominant hand.**

7. With our dominant hand, we trace a CKR over their head (+ corresponding mantra 3 times). **Visualize it entering the top of the head, then going down to the heart chakra. You need to "follow" the symbol through with your dominant hand.**

8. With our dominant hand, we trace a SHK over their head (+ corresponding mantra 3 times). **Visualize it entering the top of the head, then going down to the heart chakra. You need to "follow" the symbol through with your dominant hand.**

9. With our dominant hand, we trace a HSZSN over their head (+ corresponding mantra 3 times). **Visualize it entering the top of the head, then going down to the heart chakra. You need to "follow" the symbol through with your dominant hand.**

6.3   Step 3 - In front of the recipient

10. With our dominant hand, we trace a TDKM over their head (+ corresponding mantra 3 times). **Visualize it entering the top of the head, then going down to the solar plexus. Gently tap the top of their head 3 times (symbol activation).**

11. With our dominant hand, we trace an Usui DKM over their head (+ corresponding mantra 3 times). **Visualize it entering the top of the head, then going down to the solar plexus. Gently tap the top of their head 3 times (symbol activation).**

12. With our dominant hand, we trace a CKR over their head (+ corresponding mantra 3 times). **Visualize it entering the top of the head, then going down to the solar plexus. Gently tap the top of their head 3 times (symbol activation).**

13. With our dominant hand, we trace a SHK over their head (+ corresponding mantra 3 times). **Visualize it entering the top of the head, then going down to the solar plexus. Gently tap the top of their head 3 times (symbol activation).**

14. With our dominant hand, we trace a HSZSN over their head (+ corresponding mantra 3 times). **Visualize it entering the top of the head, then going down to the solar plexus. Gently tap the top of their head 3 times (symbol activation).**

15. Let us proceed to a slightly modified version of the Breath of Life (see dedicated chapter).

Guide the recipient with your hands:
- Raise their hands, palms up, to their head.
- Lower their hands, palms down, at plexus level.
- Bring their hands back to their head, palms facing the sky.
- Keep going, raising their hands towards the universe.

Reminder: We trace a CKR while blowing. We need to control our breath and make it last the whole Breath of Life gesture.

Universe				4
Top of the head	1		3	
Solar plexus		2		

Reminder: The Hui Yin is still contracted.

6.4 Step 4 - Behind the recipient

16. We place our hands on their shoulders. At the same time, we visualize a white sphere of light at the base of their spine, as if we were seeing it through the body and from above.

17. We inwardly state the following mantra 3 times, intending it to be received and accepted by the student's unconscious (i.e. their soul): **"You are perfectly and permanently healed, with love, trust and success, by the love of the Source."**

18. We place our thumbs together at the base of the person's skull, in the hollow of the neck, and state inwardly, **"I seal this process with love and divine grace."**

19. We visualize, at the base of their skull, a door that closes and seals itself forever. Then we trace a CHK on it to "lock" the door.

6.5 Step 5 - In front of the recipient: Transmitting accumulated energy

20. Standing about three feet away from the person, we position our hands at hip level, palms facing the student. We inhale deeply, then exhale gently, as if we were blowing a cloud of pure energy around the student. We release the **Hui Yin**. Thus, the energy accumulated throughout the initiation is released from the Hui Yin and washes over the student.

21. We end with a discreet cutting gesture (Kenyo Ku, for instance). Then, we release the person by saying something along the lines of: "Feel free to open your eyes whenever you like".

7 Self-initiation & distance initiation

7.1 Self-initiation

There are great energetic benefits to be gained from being reinitiated. We will tend to want to be initiated at Master level from now on. But here again, we need to let our intuition speak to us and put the mind aside. There is nothing demeaning about being initiated again at a lower level.

In any case, we can of course ask to share an initiation with another Master of our acquaintance.

But if we do not have the possibility of being initiated by a Master, we can perfectly initiate ourselves, or rather REinitiate ourselves.

We can either carry out the process by visualizing each symbol and gesture on ourselves, or we can use our own bodies and hands to provide more concrete "psychological" assistance.

We can also use a kind of "guinea pig", such as a stuffed toy, to represent ourselves.

7.2 Distance initiation

Conventionally and officially, we cannot initiate students remotely. In this case, it is only a question of reinitiating someone who has already been initiated and who is at a significant distance from us.

For instance, you can reinitiate your students or the students of another Master. But we cannot initiate someone at a higher level than the one they stopped at.

This is the official version and I stand by it —at least for a non-personal setting, for my intimate opinion is slightly different... Although I freely admit that I have never carried out a remote initiation.

Dear readers, dear Masters, I wish you a fruitful and luminous journey in your daily practice of Usui Reiki.

May the Source guard you and fill you with its benevolent light!

8 Usui Reiki teaching levels

According to the teachings of Mikao Usui, it is agreed that:

Level 1 (Shoden) involves the physical body

At this level, we learn the hand positions for self-treatment and treating others. We also approach the five Reiki ideals. The first principle is to capture and channel universal vital energy through the laying on of hands.

Physical healing is underway, each being progressing at their own pace.

Level 2 (Okuden) involves the mental and emotional aspects.

Level 2 significantly increases the amount of healing energy and focuses on the initiate's emotional, mental and karmic healing.

At Level 2, we are taught four symbols, according to the masters initiated by the Reiki Forum center (and four in the context of these courses in particular). They help to focus the mind on the transmission of Reiki beyond time and space, and further open up the power of Reiki. The principle is based on the ancient and universal laws governing the transfer of energy between mind and body. Using these symbols, the practitioner establishes a path through which energy flows freely between himself and the recipient.

Level 2 opens the door to even higher levels of consciousness. Our intuition grows, we become more aware of it and we understand that we need to trust its voice.

Level 3 (Shinpiden) involves consciousness and spirituality

Level 3 gives access to the Master symbol, not as an initiation to teaching, but to the use of the symbol and the mastery protocol. This level is for those who want to know everything there is to know about Reiki therapy, but do not want to become a Master Teacher.

Level 4 (Shihan) - Reiki Master Teacher

Level 4 gives the method for initiating others; it is not the end of the Reiki path, but it is the end of its first learning cycle.

It is important to note that the term "Master" has no sectarian connotations. It simply refers to the fact that we have mastered the course and that we are capable of teaching or transmitting the knowledge we have acquired.

Take time to experiment and absorb the knowledge

As with all learning, we need to fully assimilate one notion before moving on to the next. Your understanding of the past level should be complete and you should be able to navigate its steps naturally and smoothly. This applies for any level of the Reiki learning process. At the French Usui Reiki Federation, we advise you to practice and to devote at least:

> ➢ 3 months to learning between Level 1 and Level 2.
> ➢ 9 months to learning between Level 2 and Level 3.
> ➢ 6 months to learning between Level 3 and Level 4.

9 Sources

Hand movement photographs:
Personal photographs on Canon EOS 6D, retouched with Gimp 2.10 (Imac).
These illustrations are not distributable except with the author's consent: send an e-mail to hexagone.nicolas@gmail.com

Anatomical drawings
Made using Zygote, Anatomylearning and a personal modeling.
https://www.zygotebody.com/#nav=&sel=p:;h:;s:;c:0;o:0&layers=0,1,10000
http://anatomylearning.com/webgl2021v3/browser.php

Symbols:
Personal illustrations retouched with Gimp 2.10 (Imac).
These illustrations are not distributable except with the author's consent: send an e-mail to hexagone.nicolas@gmail.com

Other photographs and illustrations
Royalty-free photographs (depositphotos, stocksnap.io, pexel, pixabay...) and other unidentified artists.
Concerning the latter, if you recognize the photo of an artist that I have not been able to name, please send an e-mail to hexagone.nicolas@gmail.com, specifying the e-mail address of the artist in question, so that we can agree on how to proceed (removal of the photo or other solution).

Made in the USA
Columbia, SC
19 December 2024

50145977R00053